KINABATANGAN

CEDE PRUDENTE

SABAH COLOUR GUIDE

KINABATANGAN

Wendy Hutton

Photographs by

Cede Prudente

C.L. Chan, Wendy Hutton,
Eugene Tan and Mike Cadman

Natural History Publications (Borneo)
Kota Kinabalu
2004

Published by

NATURAL HISTORY PUBLICATIONS (BORNEO) SDN. BHD. (216807-X)

A913, 9th Floor, Phase 1, Wisma Merdeka
P.O. Box 15566
88864 Kota Kinabalu, Sabah, Malaysia
Tel: 088-233098 Fax: 088-240768
e-mail: info@nhpborneo.com
Website: www.nhpborneo.com

Sabah Colour Guide: Kinabatangan by Wendy Hutton

ISBN 983-812-093-6

First published October 2004.

Printed in Malaysia.

Contents

Foreword

The Kinabatangan, Sabah's longest river, is one of the most exciting and easily accessible places to explore the rich biodiversity of Sabah. From Kampung Abai near the river mouth, on to the major village of Sukau and further upriver as far as Batu Putih, the lower Kinabatangan offers an incredible opportunity to see a large range of wildlife including Borneo's unique proboscis monkeys, the orangutan, Bornean pygmy elephants, crocodiles, otters and countless rare and beautiful birds.

This well-illustrated book reveals the fascinating history of the lower Kinabatangan; its people, the Orang Sungei, and the plants and animals that can be discovered in its differing habitats. It also acts as a practical guide to accommodation and transport in the region, easily reached from Sandakan or Kota Kinabalu.

I feel confident that this guide, a companion to Colour Guides already published on Sandakan and Kudat, will contribute towards the development of tourism in this vitally important region.

I congratulate Wendy Hutton, the author, and Datuk C.L. Chan, the publisher, for a job well done.

Tan Sri Datuk Chong Kah Kiat

Deputy Chief Minister
and
Minister of Tourism, Culture and Environment, Sabah

CEDE PRUDENTE

Introduction

It starts deep in the heart of southwestern Sabah, where trickles spilling down from the watersheds of Trus Madi and the Maliau Basin merge with countless other rivulets to form small streams. These streams grow into the Kuamut and Milian rivers, always moving steadily to the northeast, then merge into one large river, by now the colour of *kopi susu* or milky coffee from silt washed off the sides of the steep slopes down which it flows. The volume of water increases and picks up speed as it moves ever onwards, finally threading through coastal mangroves and spilling out into the Sulu Sea. This is the Kinabatangan, at 560 km, Sabah's longest river and the second longest in all of Malaysia.

Each year, the lashing rains of the northeast monsoon cause the river to swell rapidly. Unable to disgorge into the sea quickly enough, the river frequently overflows its banks and spreads across the flat land of its lower reaches, creating a huge floodplain. The lower Kinabatangan teems with both animal and plant life,

p. vi: The Oriental Darter, frequently seen along the river, dries its wings.
Opposite: A stunning Rhinoceros Hornbill. one of 8 species which may be spotted.

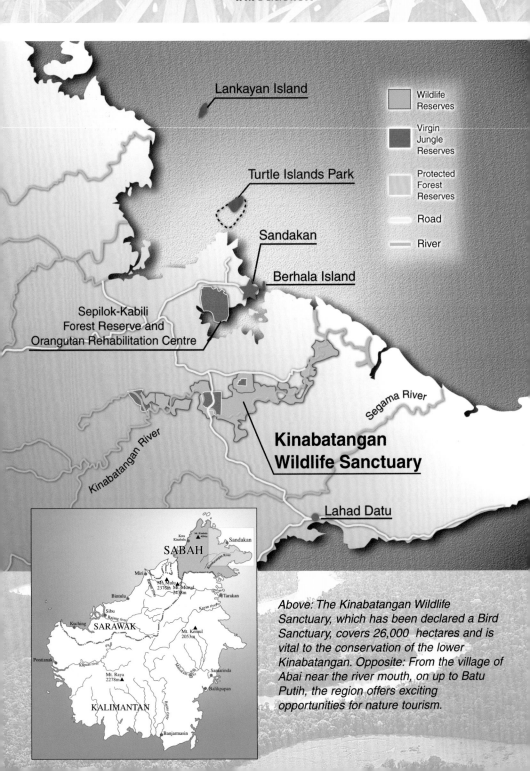

Lankayan Island

Wildlife Reserves

Virgin Jungle Reserves

Protected Forest Reserves

Road

River

Turtle Islands Park

Sandakan

Berhala Island

Sepilok-Kabili Forest Reserve and Orangutan Rehabilitation Centre

Segama River

Kinabatangan Wildlife Sanctuary

Kinabatangan River

Lahad Datu

SABAH

Kota Kinabalu

Sandakan

Miri

Mt. Mulu 2376m Mt. Murud 2438m

Bintulu

Tarakan

Sibu

Rajang river

Kuching

SARAWAK

Kayan river

Mt. Kemul 2053m

Pontianak

Kapuas river

Mt. Raya 2278m

Samarinda

Balikpapan

KALIMANTAN

Banjarmasin

Above: The Kinabatangan Wildlife Sanctuary, which has been declared a Bird Sanctuary, covers 26,000 hectares and is vital to the conservation of the lower Kinabatangan. Opposite: From the village of Abai near the river mouth, on up to Batu Putih, the region offers exciting opportunities for nature tourism.

making it the best area for viewing wildlife, not just in Sabah but in all of Southeast Asia.

For centuries, the rare treasures of Borneo's forests acted as a magnet for traders who came in search of edible birds' nests, rhinoceros horn, elephant ivory and hornbill casques for the Emperor and the wealthy mandarins of China. They also sought a hardwood resin, damar; flexible rattan vines; beeswax to make candles; fragrant woods and oil-rich illipe nuts. The mighty Kinabatangan was the only route into the forests of northeastern Sabah, to the scattered riverine settlements where forest produce and birds' nests were traded.

Today, a different form of riches draws visitors to the Kinabatangan: its remarkable wildlife and fascinating habitats which include limestone caves, dryland dipterocarp forests, riverine forest, freshwater swamp forest, oxbow lakes and salty mangrove swamps near the coast. The lower Kinabatangan offers an incredible opportunity to see a large range of wildlife including Borneo's unique Proboscis monkeys, the endearing and endangered

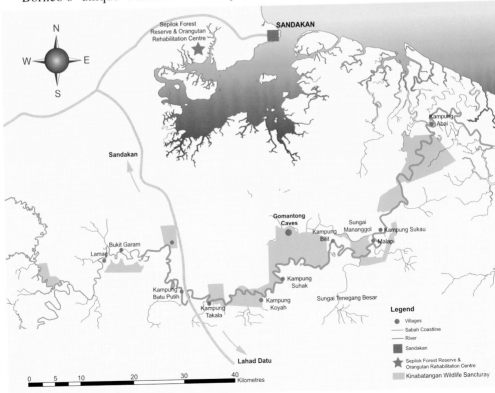

CEDE PRUDENTE

LIM CHAN KOON

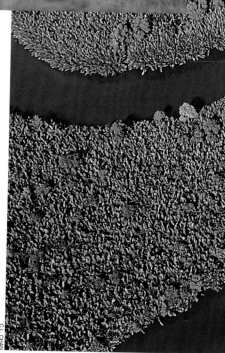

C.L. CHAN

Top: The Bornean pygmy elephant, found only in this region of Sabah.
Above: Swiftlets make their nests in Gomantong Caves. Right: The river snakes its way across the flat land, overflowing its banks each rainy season to create a floodplain.

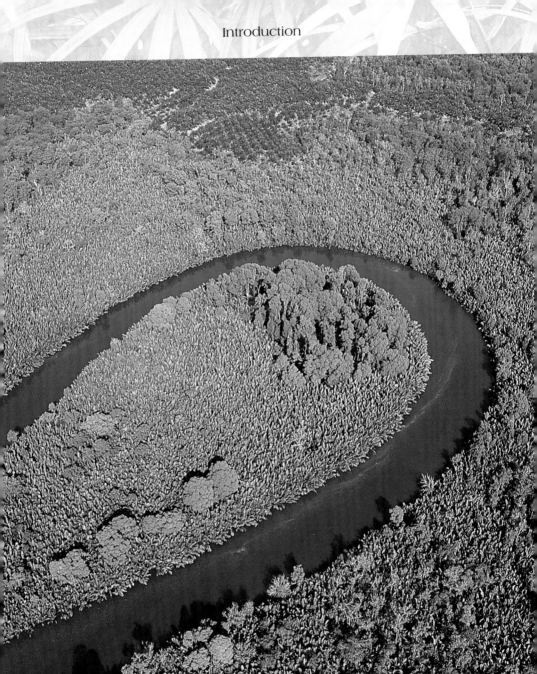

orangutan, Bornean pygmy elephants, croc-odiles, wild cats, bears, otters, wild pigs and countless rare and beautiful birds such as hornbills and the Oriental Darter.

The conservation of the Kinabatangan is vital, not only in terms of saving Sabah's wildlife but for the indigenous Orang Sungei whose lives depend on the river, and for safeguarding the region's fresh water supply. In order to protect this priceless heritage for all, the 26,000-hectare Kinabatangan Wildlife Sanctuary was declared Malaysia's first Gift to the Earth in 1999. In 2001, the Kinabatangan Wildlife Sanctuary was gazetted as a Bird Sanctuary, and work to gazette the area as a permanent wildlife sanctuary is currently underway.

CEDE PRUDENTE

WENDY HUTTON

WENDY HUTTON

CEDE PRUDENTE

C.L. CHAN

CEDE PRUDENTE

Opposite top: A large male orangutan in the wild. Opposite below: An oxbow lake. Top left: A rare shot of a Proboscis monkey drinking from the river. Top right: A typical jetty. The river yields up a couple of cat fish (right). Tortoises are also seen (above).

CEDE PRUDENTE

Timeless Route to the Treasures of Borneo

Early History of the Kinabatangan

The beginnings of human settlement along the Kinabatangan are lost in the mists of time, and the same is true for the first contact with the outside world. Although there are records of Chinese traders voyaging to the island of Borneo as long ago as the 7th century, it was not until the late 13th century that records confirm a Chinese trading expedition to the Kinabatangan.

WENDY HUTTON

Opposite: A striking sunset over the river, where even young children (above) are skilled at paddling a dugout canoe.

What's in a Name?

It is often claimed that the name "Kinabatangan" means "Chinese river", referring to the Chinese settlement which Brunei records indicate existed in the region during the 15th century. The word *batang* means river locally. However, if the name came from Chinese (*cina* or *kina*) and river (*batang*), the river would more correctly be called the Batangan Kina, because the adjective always follows the noun in local languages.

The word *"Aki"* means grandfather or ancestor in Kadazandusun, and is a prefix usually confined to gods, mountains and rivers. The first letter of *aki* is often dropped for ease of use, with *na* used as a linking prefix; Thus, Kinabalu, the mountain, is the "Solitary Father" (*balu* or *nabalu* meaning "widowed" in Kadazandusun). When it comes to the river, Aki-Na-Batangan or "Father River" has become shortened to Kinabatangan, an appropriate term for Sabah's greatest river.

At the start of the 15th century, the famous Chinese Muslim admiral, Cheng Ho, travelled to many parts of Southeast Asia and during these voyages he may well have visited the Kinabatangan. This would seem to be confirmed by the fact that the oral history of the Idahan people of Lahad Datu relates that they began trading edible birds' nests (a enormously valuable commodity) with the Chinese at this time.

A Sulu legend tells of another Chinese admiral, Ong Sum Peng, who decided to settle along the Kinabatangan near the site of Batu Putih. A small Chinese trading community grew up here as more Chinese joined him, many of them marrying local wives and becoming absorbed into the local community. The *Brunei Annals* confirm the existence of a Chinese settlement along the Kinabatangan, recording that a daughter of the first Muslim Sultan of

EUGENE TAN

WENDY HUTTON

WENDY HUTTON

Above: Ancient coffins found in the caves of Agop Batu Putih are a testament to long settlement in the region, where a Chinese trading post once existed. Left: Women sorting fish netted in an oxbow lake. Freshwater fish are a part of the staple diet, along with rice and home-grown or wild vegetables. Opposite: Huge freshwater prawns (udang galah) *are a source of income for many Orang Sungei fishermen.*

Brunei was sent to marry a Chinese in the Kinabatangan in the early 15th century (no doubt a political move to ensure a good trading relationship).

By the 18th century, the independent Sultanate of Sulu had firmly established links with China and controlled the northernmost part of Borneo. The Sultan monopolised the export of forest produce and birds' nests from the Kinabatangan, as well as pearls, dried sea cucumbers and other marine produce from the coast.

The expansionist Europeans, looking for trading opportunities in the East, turned their eyes towards the north of Borneo. There was an abortive British settlement on the island of Balambangan, off Kudat, in 1773, abandoned largely because of piracy. A century later, Baron von Overbeck negotiated with the sultans of Brunei and Sulu to obtain permanent ownership over what is now Sabah. He sold these rights to the Dent brothers, who went on to form the British North Borneo Chartered Company.

William Pryer, appointed first Resident of the East Coast in 1879, was by all accounts an energetic and competent administrator who wasted no time in visiting the Kinabatangan from his base in Sandakan. His journal records a voyage made by steamer in early 1881, noting the beautiful bright blue kingfishers and hornbills, and commenting that "everywhere along the bank, the tracks of buffaloes, deer and pigs were so abundant as to form perfect roads". However, he was shocked to find that an earlier smallpox epidemic had wiped out large numbers of people, and reported that he "steamed upriver for 90 miles (from near today's Sukau) without seeing a human being, through a country of the richest character".

W.M. POON

CEDE PRUDENTE

EUGENE TAN

Above: A young Orang Sungei man sports a traditional hat. Left: A curious male Proboscis monkey. Opposite: The entrance to a cave at Gomantong, where birds' nests are gathered.

In 300 miles, Pryer encountered only three villages. He did, however, come across large crocodiles upriver from what is now Batu Putih, describing them as "extraordinarily large and fierce, sometimes even attacking large canoes. Every month or so someone is carried off. I could hardly have believed these creatures grew so large had I not seen it."

At this time, the centre of trade for the valuable birds' nests gathered in the Gomantong caves was Kampung Melapi (not far from today's village of Sukau), where according to Pryer, other "up country produce" was also traded. The Chartered Company claimed rights over the birds' nests, taking traditional rights away from the villagers. They met with strong opposition from Melapi's headman, Pengiran Samah, who was shot dead in 1884. Perhaps due to the hostility that understandably existed in Melapi, the harvested nests were then taken overland from Gomantong to Kampung Bilit (upriver from Melapi), and shipped from there down the Kinabatangan.

The Changing Face
of the Kinabatangan

Environmental Challenges and Solutions

As foreigners looked for opportunities on Sabah's east coast in the early years of Chartered Company rule, they began applying for leases of land along the lower reaches of the Kinabatangan, accessible by boat from Sandakan. The Dutch were interested in planting tobacco (which they were already growing successfully in Java); an Australian cleared land with the intention of planting sugar, exporting the valuable hardwood timber he had felled in the process, while the Japanese established coconut plantations and later on, in 1935, a huge jute plantation in the vicinity of Kampung Bilit.

The felling of timber in the dryland dipterocarp forests along the Kinabatangan initially involved a system known as *kuda kuda* (literally "horses"), with the massive logs tipped onto a cradle and hauled along greased wooden runners—dragged by men, however, and not horses. As it was easier to remove logs from the flat land, the lower Kinabatangan area was the first to be logged on a large scale. Eventually, steam engines to help the hauling were gradually introduced, and by the 1950s, tractors were being used for logging on the hill slopes.

When the logging monopoly held by the British North Borneo Timber Company was lifted in 1952, a number of Chinese applied for timber licences and the period of intensive logging of Sabah's forests began, reaching its

Opposite: Late afternoon, Proboscis monkeys gather in the tall trees along the river banks. Above: The only bridge across the Kinabatangan, at Batu Putih.

peak in the 1970s and 1980s. During this era, countless logs felled in inland forests were towed down the Kinabatangan to the port of Sandakan for shipping overseas.

As the valuable hardwood trees began to disappear and the rate of logging declined, the development of oil palm plantations picked up pace, especially in the late 1980s and early 1990s, with many large companies from Peninsular Malaysia seeking cheaper, readily available land in Sabah. Large tracts of forest where the valuable timber had already been extracted were cleared and plantations of oil palm established.

These changes along the lower Kinabatangan pose enormous challenges to the environment. In its natural state, the Kinabatangan floodplain supports a remarkably diverse range of plants and wildlife, some species found only in this region. It also provides food and materials for the local Orang Sungei, and helps regulate the water flow and limit floods by acting as a giant sponge, soaking up the rainwater and then releasing it gradually. The floodplain also acts as a filter for water, making it suitable for further treatment as drinking water in the towns and villages around Sandakan.

C.L. CHAN

CEDE PRUDENTE

WENDY HUTTON

Wildlife lodges near Kampung Sukau, the largest village along the lower Kinabatangan, include SI Tours (opposite) and Borneo Eco Tours (above). Left: The only bridge crossing the Kinabatangan river is at Batu Putih, on the main road east to Lahad Datu and Tawau. Freshwater prawns are often sold in the simple shops near the bridge.

Right: Wildlife Expeditions was the first to build a wildlife lodge near Sukau, at the junction of the Menanggol River, a prime area for spotting proboscis monkeys. Above: The unusual sight of a Proboscis monkey taking it easy.

CEDE PRUDENTE

C.L. CHAN

The establishment of oil palm plantations in the period before adequate planning of land use was introduced has posed a severe threat to much of the Kinabatangan's valuable wildlife, resulting in isolated pockets of forest reserve too small to sustain many of the animals, and blocking traditional paths used by Sabah's elephants.

Starting in the 1980s, scientific research consistently produced evidence of the vital importance of the lower Kinabatangan in wildlife conservation. The region's potential for nature tourism was also confirmed, and by 1992 the Sabah State Government acknowledged the need to establish a conservation area along the river. Known as the Kinabatangan Wildlife Sanctuary, this consists of blocks of land linking the existing protected inland forests with the mangrove forests near the coast to provide a continuous forested corridor along the lower portion of the river, from Batu Putih down to Kampung Abai.

A project initiated by the WWF Netherlands, Partners for Wetlands, was set up in 1998. This is designed to help coordinate wetland management, conservation and restoration, with scientists, plantation owners, villagers,

CEDE PRUDENTE

Above: Proboscis Lodge near Sukau is set in spacious grounds, with comfortably furnished rooms (above left). Left: Gathering bananas from a riverside plantation. Opposite: The constantly winding of the river can result in oxbow lakes.

tourism operators and government all working together to achieve sustainable management of the lower Kinabatangan.

One of the many practical projects already underway is the replanting of the forest along the river banks. The re-establishment of indigenous species in areas which have been cleared will help prevent erosion and silting, reduce the speed of floodwaters, help filter chemicals which run off from the oil palm estates and improve river fisheries, not just through ensuring cleaner water but as a result of ripe fruits dropping from the trees into the river. thus providing food for the fish.

Nature tourism to the lower Kinabatangan increased dramatically in just one decade, as news of its rich wildlife and greater accessibility spread. The first basic jungle camp was established in 1989 downriver from Batu Putih, near an oxbow lake known as Danau Girang, while the first wildlife lodge in Sukau was established in 1991. From the handful of visitors who came across Sandakan Bay to Suan Lamba by boat, then voyaged by Landrover along a track into the sole lodge in Sukau in the beginning, the number of wildlife operators with lodges near Sukau has grown to six and the number of visitors to Sukau swelled to around 13,000 in 2000.

WENDY HUTTON

The People of the River

hen the British came to Sabah, they not only changed its name to British North Borneo but decided to call the various communities living along the Kinabatangan river by just one name. With faultless logic, they named them Orang Sungei or "People of the River".

The twenty or so ethnic groups now classified as Orang Sungei share much in terms of lifestyle and culture. Although the majority are Muslim, some follow the Christian religion.

They are far from being one homogenous group, speaking languages belonging to two different linguistic families, the Dusunic and the Paitanic. Most of the Orang Sungei of the lower Kinabatangan speak a language they call Sungei, which is is a Dusunic language classified as a dialect of Eastern Kadazan. (This Eastern Kadazan language group also includes people from the Labuk Bay area, as well as Dusuns from the Segama, all of whom refer to themselves as Orang Sungei.)

Five Orang Sungei groups living in the upper Kinabatangan (the Sinabu, Sinarupa, Kalabuan, Makian and Kumanau) speak dialects of a Paitanic language (as indeed, do the Muslim Idahan of Lahad Datu). To further complicate the picture, people living along the Kinabatangan have, over the centuries, intermarried with other indigenous people as well as with immigrant groups who established themselves in northeastern Sabah, such as the Suluk, Bugis, Cagayan and Chinese.

The Orang Sungei—who have never been numerous—live in small settlements scattered along the Kinabatangan. Until

The Orang Sungei include many different ethnic groups, most of whom make their living by fishing the lakes and rivers.

WENDY HUTTON

Terrunggari the White Crocodile

There are many legends among the Orang Sungei featuring the crocodile, a huge reptile that still can be seen along the banks of the Kinabatangan and which has always commanded respect from mankind. One of these tales, related by the elders of Bukit Garam to Shim Phyau Soon, claims peaceful co-existence between the Orang Sungei and the estuarine crocodile. According to this story, in the days when crocodiles never attacked the village folk and also had the ability to speak, there was an enormous white crocodile living in the Kinabatangan. One of the village children, while swimming in the river, was suddenly taken by this crocodile, named Terrunggari. He dragged the boy to the mouth of the Kinabatangan, saying he did not intend to hurt him but wanted the boy to watch a duel he was going to fight with another massive crocodile named Berlintang.

Berlintang ruled the sea, but also wanted to control the rivers and thus be able to attack and eat all the animals and humans living along their banks. Terrunggari, the white crocodile, told the boy before the battle that if he saw red blood coming to the surface of the river, it would mean Terrunggari had won. However, if he saw white blood, it would mean Terrunggari had been defeated by Berlintang and the boy should then run and warn everyone in his village that they were no longer safe, as Berlintang and all the crocodiles from the sea would attack them. He also told the boy that he could recognise the sea crocodiles because they had only four toes, whereas he, Terrunggari, and the other river crocodiles had five toes.

The battle between the two crocodiles took place, and eventually, when red blood was seen and the body of the dead Berlintang floated to the surface, the boy realised that Terrunggari and his river crocodiles had won the right to stay in the river. This meant that he and his kind would continue to co-exist peacefully with man. (Despite this charming tale, co-existence remained more in the realm of myth than reality, according to early travellers who reported that "every month or so", someone along the Kinabatangan was taken by a crocodile.)

Local fishermen are skilled at throwing a circular cast net (p. 23), as well as fashioning and placing various types of trap (left) to catch fish and prawns(above). Local children (above left) are sometimes shy.

the 19th century, there were only three ethnic groups in the lower part of the river: the Sukang near Batu Putih; the Buludupies at Melapi and the Sabangan at Sukau. Idahans from Lahad Datu migrated to Melapi in the 1880s, some moving on to Sukau, joined later by Liwagu people from the upper Kinabatangan.

The Sabangan settled between Melapi and Sukau, then 30 Sabangan families moved downriver to found the settlement of Abai. Sukang groups from upriver moved to Lamag, then to Bukit Garam and down to Batu Putih. Today, Orang Sungei are still found upriver beyond Batu Putih, as well as along tributaries of the Kinabatangan, Sungei Lamag and Sungei Lokan.

Naturally, the lives of the Orang Sungei are focused around the river, which provides a means of communication as well as a vital source of food with fish and freshwater prawns, which are also caught in the oxbow lakes of the lower Kinabatangan. Recognising the demand for the excellent freshwater prawns (*udang galah*) and fish, many Orang Sungei now catch these to sell to palm oil estates, to tourist lodges or to small shops selling to passing motorists near the Kinabatangan bridge at Batu Putih.

Fish and prawn traps (*bubu*) made from rattan and split bamboo (or, downriver in Abai, of nipah) are fashioned by hand and positioned in the rivers and streams. In addition, the men are skilled at throwing cast nets (*rambat*), as well as fixing trammel nets (*pukat*), leaving them in position and checking them regularly for fish. Many varieties of freshwater fish are found, including the highly prized goby known by its Chinese name, *soon hock*. Several varieties of catfish (*ikan patin*) are common, the flesh of the best ones fine textured and sweet. If a large number of live fish is caught, they are sometimes kept for up to two weeks in a cage in the river, under a shady landing platform in front

Sorting prawns at Kampung Abai (above). Most local houses are build of wood, with some near Kampung Abai fashioned from nipah thatch (opposite, below).

WENDY HUTTON

WENDY HUTTON

of the house, ensuring a constant supply of fresh fish.

The Orang Sungei have long used the forests of the Kinabatangan as a source of building material, firewood, food and medicine. Even today, they gather wild plants to eat as vegetables, including various types of fern growing near the river banks. Some Orang Sungei still plant rice, relying upon the annual rains to water the crop. Many families plant a small orchard near their homes, selling any surplus fruits at the nearest weekly *tamu* or market. In locations where elephants are not regular visitors, some Orang Sungei have established banana plantations.

Wild foods are supplemented with edible young leaves from tapioca, papaya, sweet potato and other crops

EUGENE TAN

Many local homes have well kept gardens (left), even though the kitchens may still be simple (above). The trunk of a giant Koompassia *tree (opposite, right) bears stakes hammered in to allow men to scale the tree to gather wild honey; these stakes have now become permanently embedded. Opposite, left: A still backwater not far from Kampung Bilit, which can be reached by both road and river.*

EUGENE TAN

planted in *kampung* gardens. In fact, with wild or home-grown vegetables, spanking fresh fish or freshwater prawns, rice and tasty condiments or *sambal*, one can dine superbly in an Orang Sungei home.

Orang Sungei houses are generally built of unpainted wood and covered with corrugated zinc roofing; many are surprisingly large and roomy, with high ceilings. In front of the houses, and built on the river's edge, is the family bathroom, laundry and boat landing stage. Usually reached by solid wooden planks laid on the river bank, this structure consists of two or three massive logs kept in position by wires or rope. A small wooden shed with a partially planked floor sits astride the logs and serves as the washing area and toilet. (Many houses, however, now have modern toilets, or have been provided with bright blue plastic module toilets by the Health Department.)

CEDE PRUDENTE

The Ever-changing River

Different Environments along the Kinabatangan

As the Kinabatangan snakes its way through the flat land of its lower reaches, it gives the impression of timelessness, of flowing endlessly and never changing. Nothing could be further from the truth, for with each rainy season, the river rises and spreads over the floodplain, then recedes. Over the centuries, the relentless flow of water against the curving edges of some of its tightest bends gradually washes away the banks, and the river breaks through to flow in a relatively straight

CEDE PRUDENTE

CEDE PRUDENTE

line. The curving loop of water (once its main course) is very gradually separated from the new line of river by the build-up of silt, forming what is known as an oxbow lake. There are around 20 oxbow lakes (*danau*) in the lower Kinabatangan, most of them accessible by small boat during the rainy season when river channels cut through from the main river to the lake. At other times, tracks through the forest to the lake can be followed on foot.

The oxbow lakes are a popular place for the Orang Sungei to fish, but they are not the only ones busy doing this. The lakes are paradise for water birds such as egrets, herons and the Oriental darter, not forgetting the ubiquitous kingfishers. Another creature attracted by the fish in these lakes is the flat-headed cat, while otters can also be seen. Deer and wild pigs are often found around the oxbow lakes, as well as Proboscis monkeys.

Riverine forest, lining the banks of the river (above the lowest reaches which are affected by saline water from the sea) is the type most commonly seen by visitors as they cruise along the Kinabatangan from around Abai up to Batu Putih. Figs and other trees which need plenty of light predominate, while along the river and channels leading to the oxbow lakes, the beautiful purple-flowered *Lagerstroemia* can often be sighted.

It is a remarkable experience to cruise slowly by boat through a freshwater swamp forest flooded by seasonal rains. Tall trees with pleated trunks stand firmly, their buttress roots invisible under the floodwaters; these

A male Proboscis monkey (p. 30) is an impressive sight. Oxbow lakes (p. 31) provide quiet havens where wildlife is often seen. The changing face of the river at sunrise (p. 32–33) and at sunset (p. 34–35). An endemic form of Phalaenopsis amabilis *(above) and* Hoya *(right) found only in the Kinabatangan.*

same trees, in the dry season, will be left high and dry. The trees growing at the edge of rivers and lakes are especially adapted to cope with periodic flooding, while the vegetation growing in permanently waterlogged areas tends to be low shrubs and grasses.

The dryland forests of the lower Kinabatangan are, not surprisingly, further from the river and its annual floods. As these forests contain the valuable timber species, dipterocarps, they have virtually disappeared except in some of the forest reserves. Owing to their small size, these forests are no longer populated by large numbers of primates, although some orangutan and gibbons may still be found here.

Towards the mouth of the river, below Abai, the river water becomes brackish, owing to the influx of sea water at high tide, with very few plants able to survive in this environment. The most striking are the various species of mangrove, all having cleverly adapted roots which allow them to absorb oxygen when the water rises. Also found in brackish water are stands of nipah palms, These are particularly useful to the Orang Sungei, as their dried leaves can be used as a roofing material, the ripe nipah fruits eaten, and the sap drawn from the inflorescence turned into palm sugar.

Living Treasures of the Kinabatangan

Southeast Asia's Most Remarkable Wildlife

Huge male proboscis monkeys crash noisily as they leap dramatically from tree to tree, seemingly having leapt before they looked. Below, a crocodile basks in the mud of the river bank, perhaps musing on his chances of grabbing a meal from among the troop of macaques noisily fossicking for small crabs not far away. A solitary orangutan sitting high in a tree ignores the pair of vividly coloured Rhinoceros Hornbills whooshing overhead, while the rare Oriental Darter dives like a rapier into the river and swims underwater to spear a fish.

CEDE PRUDENTE

CEDE PRUDENTE

The rare Storm's Stork (p. 38) can sometimes be seen near the river or the oxbow lakes. Proboscis monkeys, found only in Borneo, are sociable animals living in harems of females and juveniles (p. 39) dominated by an alpha male (below). Young male monkeys tend to form small groups. Male adults are significantly larger than the females, and sport a huge fleshy nose and pot belly.

These are just some of the astonishing animals and birds which can be seen while cruising on the Kinabatangan and its tributaries, or along the narrow channels cutting through the forest to secluded oxbow lakes. Even with the current challenges posed by the loss or fragmentation of their habitat, the wildlife of the lower Kinabatangan is exceptional. And what's more, it is remarkably accessible to the nature tourist.

One of the star attractions for many visitors is the remarkable **Proboscis monkey**, found only in Borneo. Although groups of these monkeys live in coastal areas and swamps in other parts of Sabah, the biggest concentration is found in the lower Kinabatangan, particularly around Sukau and the Menanggol River.

CEDE PRUDENTE

CEDE PRUDENTE

Crocodiles (above) are frequently seen basking on the muddy banks, while curious otters (right) are best spotted at the oxbow lakes.
Channels cutting through the forest to oxbow lakes (opposite left) are often rich in birdlife such as hornbills (opposite, top & bottom) and woodpeckers (opposite, centre).

CEDE PRUDENTE

CEDE PRUDENTE

CEDE PRUDENTE

C.L. CHAN

Leeches (right) are only rarely encountered. Clouds of colourful butterflies, which feed on animal urine, can often be seen in cleared patches of forest (below). Sightings of the endemic Borneo pygmy elephant (overleaf) are particularly exciting. Sukau and Bilit are usually he best places to spot elephants.

CEDE PRUDENTE

CEDE PRUDENTE

C.L. CHAN

Those with sharp eyes who take the time to study the vegetation while trekking will see a rich variety of colourful insects and spiders.

CEDE PRUDENTE

CEDE PRUDENTE

CEDE PRUDENTE

CEDE PRUDENTE

CEDE PRUDENTE

CEDE PRUDENTE

The Proboscis monkey—especially the male, which is considerably larger than the female—is one of the most bizarre creatures of the forest. As the name implies, the male has a truly huge, dangling fleshy nose, a large pot belly (all the better to digest his diet of leaves), a thick long white tail, a ginger flat-top hair style which a rap singer might envy, and thick body fur graduating from pale red through beige and grey to white. A dominant male gathers around him a harem of females (easily recognisable by their smaller size, delicate upturned noses and grey tails) and juveniles, noisily warning any cheeky young males from the bachelor packs to stay away.

CEDE PRUDENTE

Some of the primates which may be seen in the forests along the Kinabatangan include gibbons (above), pig-tailed macaques (opposite, top left), the appealing Slow Loris (opposite, bottom left) and the Proboscis monkey (opposite, bottom right). The closest relative of the tiny shy mousedeer (opposite, top right) is, surprisingly, the elephant. A Storm's Stork scans the river for fish (top).

Proboscis monkeys always come down to the edge of rivers or oxbow lakes in the late afternoon for a final feed and a little socialising before going to sleep in the trees. They can also be spotted here as they awake in the morning, slowly easing into the day before heading off into the forest away from the river. Cruising quietly in an open boat in the late afternoon or early morning is an ideal way of spotting these entertaining monkeys.

Far less commonly seen is the **orangutan**, the highly intelligent, gentle red ape found only in Borneo and Sumatra. Endangered largely through loss of habitat, these animals tend to live solitary lives, although the female will keep her young beside her for up to six years, until it becomes sexually mature. The orangutan builds a fresh nest of broken branches and leaves high in a tree (the most popular variety being the *laran*) every evening. While these nests can often be seen, to catch sight of the animals themselves is less easy. However, when fig trees are fruiting, these are a good spot for catching sight of birds and sometimes of orangutan enjoying a feast.

The lower Kinabatangan and the Danum Valley in the southeast of Sabah are the only two places in the world where it is possible to see ten different primates. Apart from the orangutan and Proboscis monkeys, there are the smaller leaf monkeys or **langgurs**. With their delicate faces and fine long

Bearded pigs can often be seen around Danau Girang.

CEDE PRUDENTE

Saving the Orangutan

It is estimated that 80–90% of Sabah's orangutan population lives in disturbed forests outside protected areas (even though the animal itself is strictly protected by law). HUTAN, the first project to ever study orangutan behaviour in degraded or disturbed forests, was established in 1998. Its office is based in Sukau, with the study area in a forest reserve a short distance downriver.

HUTAN is (among other tasks) studying orangutan adaptation to disturbed forests with a view to designing a management programme for the population living outside protected areas. The organisation is also conducting a state-wide census of orangutan, and working to diminish conflict between humans and orangutan and elephants. This is particularly important as the encroachment of oil palm plantations on the traditional feeding areas of the elephants has led to problems not only with plantation owners but with the villagers, whose gardens are sometimes ravaged by herds of elephants.

Recognising the need to involve the local population in the conservation of the orangutan, a tourism project has been established, where locals brief visitors on the research in progress and guide them to view the animals in the wild. This tourism initiative, which was established in late 2003, is linked with the Sukau homestay programme, thus achieving maximum local participation.

CEDE PRUDENTE

Female Proboscis monkeys (above) are easily recognised by their smaller size and dainty, upturned noses. The striking male (right) has a thick white tail and is remarkably agile, despite its size.

CEDE PRUDENTE

CEDE PRUDENTE

hair, the langgurs are particularly attractive. Perhaps the most beautiful is the silver langgur, whose young have bright auburn body fur with winsome black faces and white fur covering their heads. Very similar but without the metallic sheen of the silver langgur, the grey or Hose's langgur, and the reddish or maroon langgur can also be seen; it is not unusual to spot the silver langgur along the banks of the Kinabatangan not far upriver from Sukau.

Another of the primates which may be encountered in the dipterocarp forests of the Kinabatangan is the Bornean **gibbon**, whose magical early morning call is absolutely unmistakable. However, only the lucky few will catch sight of this long-armed ape, which swings rapidly like a pendulum between the branches.

The **tarsier**—a nocturnal primate with enormous round eyes, a long tail and a head that can swivel 270 degrees—seems to have been the inspiration for the extra-terrestrial film character, ET. Another nocturnal primate found in the lower Kinabatangan rainforest is the **slow loris**, whose huge eyes, furry body and gentle (not to say downright slow) movements make it a favourite with all who see it.

While macaques (right) are common, beautiful silver and red leaf monkeys (langgurs) are also found in the forest (below). A herd of elephants crossing the river in search of food (opposite).

CEDE PRUDENTE

C.L. CHAN

To complete the list of primates found in the Kinabatangan are the long-tailed or crab-eating **macaques** and larger pig-tailed macaques. The former live in noisy troupes, and are particularly social animals with little fear of man. It is easy to observe them almost everywhere along the Kinabatangan, on the muddy banks as well as in the trees.

In Sabah, a sub-species of the Asian **elephant**—smaller than its African counterpart—is found only in the east of the state, and particularly around the Kinabatangan. Scientists were initially unable to decide if these elephants are descended from some given as a gift to the Sultan of Sulu (who received them from either the Sultan of Brunei or the King of Thailand, and left them in Sabah). Another theory was that they are the remnants of elephants which came from Asia during the Ice Ages, when Borneo was linked by land bridges with the Asian mainland.

It has recently been shown through DNA studies, however, that the elephants found in Sabah and eastern Kalimantan are actually a distinct sub-species known as the Bornean pygmy elephant. These are smaller, with relatively larger ears and longer tails than mainland Asian elephants. It is now thought Borneo's elephants became isolated from other Asian elephants as long as 300,000 years ago, and are now confined to Sabah's east coast because it is the only region which offers natural salt licks.

CEDE PRUDENTE

As much of their traditional territory has now been occupied by oil palm plantations—whose young palms make a very tasty treat—the elephants have come into frequent conflict with man in the past two or three decades. It has been estimated that only around 150 elephants still remain in the lower Kinabatangan, most commonly seen around Sukau, Bilit and Bukit Garam. Elephants are creatures of habit and always return to the same areas to feed or congregate; local guides will be able to point out where it might be possible to catch sight of these endangered mammals.

Because most of the Orang Sungei living along the river are Muslim and therefore do not eat pork, there is still a reasonable population of **bearded pigs** in the lower Kinabatangan. Other mammals such as **wild cats** (including

C. L. CHAN

the beautifully patterned clouded leopard and civets), the **sun bear** and **deer** can all be found in the forests and sometimes even seen raiding the plantations of the region.

Bird watchers will be richly rewarded by a visit to the lower Kinabatangan, but it's not only the enthusiast who will be impressed by the variety and brilliance of the **birdlife**. Depending on the particular habitat, it is possible to see such water birds as slender white egrets, the Black-crowned Night Heron, the rare Storm's Stork and the endangered Oriental Darter or snake bird, which has already disappeared from the freshwater swamps of Peninsular Malaysia.

Several species of kingfisher, each more vividly coloured than the last, are often seen and heard shrieking their way across the river. The large Stork-billed Kingfisher with its orange beak, and the tiny metallic Blue-eared Kingfisher are the two most commonly spotted. Scarlet Broadbills; the huge and solemn Buffy Fish Owl (which is particularly easy to spot with a light at night); the impressive Brahminy Kite, with its white head and auburn wings; several varieties of spectacular hornbills with their huge casques and the Crested Serpent Eagle (which can sometimes be seen lurking near the Gomantong Caves) are just some of the almost 200 bird species recorded in the lower Kinabatangan.

CEDE PRUDENTE

CEDE PRUDENTE

CEDE PRUDENTE

CEDE PRUDENTE

A Leopard Cat (p. 58). Sun Bear (p. 59, top) and tree shrew (p. 59 below) pale into insignificance in size when compared with the Bornean pygmy elephant—which certainly looms large when seen face to face (p. 56–57). The rich birdlife includes the Oriental Pied Hornbill (above) and the Crested Goshawk (left & opposite right). Other species shown here are the Black-and-red Broadbill (opposite, top left); the striking Stork-billed Kingfisher (opposite, left centre) and the Dusky Munia (opposite, below left)

CEDE PRUDENTE

CEDE PRUDENTE

CEDE PRUDENTE

CEDE PRUDENTE

ARTHUR Y.C. CHUNG

Monitor lizards (top), turtles and tortoises (above) are among the reptiles found in the Kinabatangan. Snakes (opposite, below) can often be seen coiled in the trees overhanging the river banks, while the magnificent Brahminy Kite dominates the skies (opposite, top).

Estuarine **crocodiles** are the largest reptiles that can be seen along the rivers; they are easily spotted at night with a light, and can sometimes be seen lying on the muddy banks of the river, especially in the early morning. You may need the help of a sharp-eyed guide to spot some of the **frogs** found on the river banks or along riverside trails, and could be lucky enough to spot a dwarf frog no bigger than your smallest fingernail, or see Malaysia's largest frog (*Rana malesiana*). **Snakes** can often be spotted coiled in the branches of trees hanging over the river. Freshwater **terrapins** and **tortoises** are difficult to spot, but visitors often catch sight of the large **monitor lizards** that often scavenge along the river bank.

CEDE PRUDENTE

Exploring the
Kinabatangan

*For anyone fond of sport or natural history, I cannot
imagine a pleasanter ... trip than floating down the Kina
Batangan ... and stopping at any spot required.*

— W.B. Pryer, 1881

The wildlife of the lower Kinabatangan is acknowledged by experts to be the most varied and easily accessible in all of Southeast Asia. Over the past decade, increasing numbers of visitors have come to discover the rich bird and animal life, as well as the intriguing forests near the river. Recently, there have been a number of initiatives to introduce visitors to the culture of the local Orang Sungei as well.

Currently, most nature tourism is concentrated around Sukau, accessible by road and offering comfortable accommodation to visitors prepared to pay for well-managed package tours. In an effort to encourage sustainable tourism and to distribute the economic benefits of tourism among the Orang Sungei, as well as to remove the stress of too many visitors in one location, other areas are being opened up to tourism with accommodation, transport and guiding services provided by the indigenous Orang Sungei.

Visitors prepared to travel slightly off the beaten track will be rewarded by the opportunity to view the wildlife in less crowded conditions, to get to know the lifestyle of the local people, and to know that they are helping to make tourism a sustainable activity by encouraging the Orang Sungei to benefit from nature tourism and thus be even more committed to the preservation of Kinabatangan's wildlife.

At the moment, the villages upriver of Batu Putih do not offer facilities for tourism. Although this area is reputed to contain some of the most attractive forests, channels and lakes found along the river, exploring the upper Kinabatangan requires more logistical planning than most visitors are able to accomplish. This guide, therefore, concentrates on the lower Kinabatangan from Batu Putih on down to Kampung Abai, towards the mouth of the river.

The area referred to as **Batu Putih** consists of several small villages (Kampung Mengaris, Kampung Paris and Kampung Perpaduan), as well as the main village of Kampung Batu Putih—in total, a population of around 1,500. Until the bridge (the only one across the entire length of the river) was constructed in 1986, the Kinabatangan was crossed at this point by a vehicular ferry which winched itself back and forth on chains. A number of small shops near the bridge sell large freshwater prawns (*udang galah*) and river fish, while there is a large coffee shop with drinks and a good range of food on the Lahad Datu side of the bridge.

Shortly before the bridge, a striking white limestone finger stabs upwards. Surely this is the "White Rock" or Batu Putih? In fact, it is not. The white rock after which the area is named is an insignificant stone near the river at the base of Bukit Mensuli, on the Lahad Datu side of the bridge. The dramatic limestone hill is **Agop Batu Tulug**, where caves house some of the most important archaeological remains found in all of Sabah.

Trekking through the forest (p. 66). Above: Ancient coffins at Agop Batu Tulug are found in caves in a limestone outcrop (opposite). Typical homestay houses (p. 70-71) where a warm welcome awaits.

MINI MUZIUM
GUA BATU TULUG
KINABATANGAN
SANDAKAN

CEDE PRUDENTE

Cave burials are a feature of many societies in Southeast Asia, and in an area prone to flooding like the lower Kinabatangan, it is not surprising that places safe above the level of the floodwaters should have been used for storing coffins. What is surprising is the incredible challenge of hefting massive wooden coffins (many of them made of heavy ironwood or *belian*) up the vertical hill to the safety of caves piercing its upper level.

The coffins of Batu Tulug were recorded as early as 1894 by British working in the region, but it was only when the Sabah Museum excavated the site and examined the coffins that their contents became known. Apart from typical Borneo objects such as blowpipes, spears and gongs, Chinese artifacts and porcelain were also discovered.

It is speculated that the Batu Tulug caves may first have been used by the early Chinese traders during the 15th century, as the Chinese place great importance on their final resting place. Although this may well be the case, cave and cliff burials are known in other Orang Sungei areas (such as Danum Valley and near Kampung Lokan, further up the Kinabatangan), so the idea of cave burials was obviously not adopted from the Chinese—it was, in fact, probably the other way around.

Sabah Museum has constructed a series of wooden staircases leading up the sheer, 40-metre limestone hill, making a once exceptionally difficult climb far less demanding. There are two main caves containing coffins, which are estimated to be 200–250 years old. The hardwood coffins in the

M.C. CADMAN

lowest cave are relatively simple, usually with carved buffalo heads at the front, some having intricate incised designs on the lid. Further up, the Sawat cave reveals more refined carving on the coffins, with crocodiles, lizards and snakes. Those prepared to make the final scramble over jagged limestone to the summit on the way to Agop Sawat will be rewarded with a great view over the surrounding landscape, with a glimpse of the river snaking through.

Unfortunately, the contents of the Information Centre of the Agop Batu Tulug Museum have not yet been put in place, so it is currently not possible for interested visitors to find out more about this important site.

Batu Putih is the location of MESCOT (Model Ecologically Sustainable Community Tourism), a community effort involving the local Orang Sungei in eco-tourism. Initially funded and assisted by WWF Norway in 1997, the project involved the villagers in planning and training programmes, and they themselves now run a number of projects, coordinated by the youthful and energetic Mohammed Hashim Abdul Hamid (a local Orang Sungei). These projects include the **Miso Walai Homestay Programme**, a boat service for wildlife viewing, a wildlife lodge nearby, a forest rehabilitation programme, a handicraft association, a kayaking club (for the use of the locals only) and an ethnobotany partnership.

The homestay programme is the longest running and one of the best managed in Sabah, involving around 20 families whose houses have been approved for receiving visitors. Thanks to computer training and English language courses, the Miso Walai's internet booking system works well, and foreign visitors to the homes scattered in the villages around Batu Putih will be able to communicate with their host families.

In order to spread the tourism equitably, it is not possible for visitors to choose the host family and village, as this is done on a roster system. It must be admitted that the villages around Batu Putih are not the most attractive along the Kinabatangan, largely due to their proximity to the main Lahad Datu road. However, even if the homes are not in the most pleasant surroundings, they are increasingly beautified with flowering shrubs and pot plants, and the warm welcome more than compensates for the location.

Activities are chosen to suit the visitor's interests and can include wildlife viewing, visiting the caves of Agop Batu Tulug; looking for wildlife while cruising along the river; learning to fish local style; helping plant trees along the river bank as part of the reforestation project; walking the trail along the ridge through undisturbed dipterocarp forest on Bukit Masuli (protected by Sabah Forest Development Authority); attending a cultural night or a mock Orang Sungei wedding; spending a night or two in the wildlife lodge near an oxbow lake or even learning how to cook some of the local dishes. Recently, a permanent jungle lodge was built near Danau Kaboi and run as part of the MESCOT project.

The first place to offer somewhere along the Kinabatangan to experience the remarkable wildlife in the surrounding forest, oxbow lakes, river channels and the main river itself, **Uncle Tan's Jungle Camp** at Danau Girang has

CEDE PRUDENTE

achieved almost legendary status among budget travellers. In 1989, Tan Su Lim (known to all as Uncle Tan) was given permission to use the area around the oxbow lake, **Danau Girang**, as well as two smaller adjacent lakes, as a base for tourism activities. He was also made an honorary ranger.

A qualified tour guide and a passionate environmentalist, Uncle Tan built an extremely basic camp in order to have minimal impact on the environment, and offered his simple facilities and guiding services at a very low price. Uncle Tan passed away in 2002, but his famous camp (about 30 minutes down river from the Kinabatangan bridge at Batu Putih) is still being run by his family, and upgrading operations have considerably improved the level of comfort.

What makes this place different from other Kinabatangan lodges (apart from its very basic facilities and remarkable atmosphere of conviviality among the staff and guests) is its location right in the midst of the forest, at

M.C. CADMAN

M.C. CADMAN

The riverside setting of most wildlife lodges offers a pleasant place to watch the passing parade (left). Traditional dugout canoes (above) are largely replaced by sawn timber boats today. The narrow Menanggol River (opposite) is a favourite site for viewing Proboscis monkeys, which can also be seen along the Kinabatangan itself, and by some of the oxbow lakes.

the edge of an oxbow lake rather than on the banks of the Kinabatangan. During the dry season, it is about a 10-minute walk from the river landing stage to the camp. However, when the river floods and fills the channels winding through the forest to a series of oxbow lakes, it is a thrilling journey by boat through the gloomy flooded forest to Danau Girang, where trees adapted to seasonal flooding stand surrounded by water.

From the camp, it is possible to walk along forest trails where a wide

Set beside an oxbow lake which floods the surrounding forest during the rainy season (opposite), Uncle Tan's is known for the many animals and birds nearby, include egrets (right) and hornbills (above).

range of wildlife can be spotted, or to sit quietly at the edge of Danau Girang to observe the birds and maybe even catch sight of otters. The normally shy orangutan has been known to come right into the campsite, while bearded pigs and monitor lizards are constant visitors near the kitchen area, with civets sometimes making an evening appearance.

Early morning, dusk and night-time boat safaris along the Kinabatangan itself reveal countless birds, crocodiles and groups of Proboscis monkeys (though rarely in the concentration often found along the Menanggol near Sukau), while elephants often visit the facilities built by the Wildlife Department in the forest on the opposite side of Danau Girang.

On the other side of the Kinabatangan, Danau Usu can be reached after a 10–15 minute hike. This oxbow lake is rich in wildlife, with plentiful deer, pig and wild cat and even crocodile prints visible in the mud, as well as many hornbills and Oriental Darters. Overnight camping trips can be arranged near Danau Usu in the dry season.

Kampung Bilit (which takes its name from the tall white-trunked *kabilit* trees in the nearby lowland forests) actually feels more remote than it really is. Situated on a gentle curve of the Kinabatangan about 25 km upriver from Sukau, Bilit is accessible by a 4.5-km road leading in from the main Gomantong–Sukau road, 9 km before Sukau. Perhaps it is the small size of the village—currently a mere 150 people living in 26 houses—that gives it a somewhat isolated feeling. The upriver portion of the village, where spacious wooden houses with flower-filled gardens nestle in the shade of some towering *belunu* (wild mango) trees, is particularly attractive.

Bilit has still has traces of its past: the shell of an old British North Borneo Company building stands next to the small village mosque; the remains of the large Japanese jute plantation, Shoko San Kai Sha, can be seen about 20 minutes downriver, and there is a memorial to British forces who had an observation post on the top of the nearby hill, Bukit Belanda, during WWII. Some of the older men still know the whereabouts of the trail to Gomantong, used in the early years of the British North Borneo Company to bring the valuable edible birds' nests to Bilit then downriver to Sandakan.

The villagers of Bilit, like almost all Orang Sungei, make their living from fishing in the river and the nearby oxbow lake, Danau Bilit. This lake is a perfect oxbow shape, unfortunately appreciated only from the air, and is accessible by boat during the rainy season. At other times, it takes less than 5 minutes by boat from the village to the start of a trail, where a walk of 20–25 minutes finishes at a solid roofed platform jutting out over the lake. For some reason, this trail seems to be one of the few areas along the Kinabatangan frequented by leeches.

Incredible as it may seem, the villagers have a photograph to prove that it is possible to water ski on Danau Bilit, and they swear that it is perfectly safe for swimming as crocodiles have never been seen there. But there certainly are other reptiles, such as large monitor lizards which swim casually across the lake.

Bilit is an area traditionally used by elephants, and the establishment of a nearby oil palm plantation has diminished the elephants' feeding area. An electrified fence surrounding this plantation keeps the elephants from venturing in to uproot the tender young palms, forcing them to look elsewhere for food. Noticing how the elephants scrupulously avoid going near the electrified wire, the villagers have strung an old wire (non-electrified, but who's going to tell the elephants that?) at one end of village street, to prevent the elephants coming in to their gardens. So far, the system is working (though the smart elephants may eventually figure it out).

An even more imaginative approach is also being tried. Once a week, the men of the village set aside time to plant bananas in three widely separated

C.L. CHAN

A Long-tailed Parakeet (above) and a Black-and-yellow Broadbill (below) are two birds commonly found in the region. Most safaris are done in open locally made boats (opposite).

plantations to provide food for the elephants, reasoning that it will keep them away from village gardens and also attract the elephants on a regular basis (all the better for nature tourism). They are also planning to plant two species of tree in the area near the village: the *laran*, the tree favoured by orang-utan for building their sleeping nests, and the *binuang*, where hornbills particularly like to rest.

The villagers of Bilit have fought fiercely to defend the beautiful virgin forest of Bukit Belanda, a 420-metre hill just behind the village classified as *kampung* land. This forest contains precious hardwood trees sought by the logging industry, but the villagers want to maintain the forest as a haven for wildlife. Although it was British soldiers who maintained a look-out on this hill, the name Bukit Belanda or Dutch Hill came into use when Holland was briefly in charge of North Borneo during the last war.

The climb to the summit, where a simple marker was erected in 1956, takes 40–45 minutes. The ideal time for climbing is around 6 am, when the day is still cool and the view from the summit is often superb: the river snaking its way down to the sea, forests interspersed with plantations pierced by occasional limestone outcrops draped with shreds of early-morning mist and—if you're fortunate—Mount Kinabalu, far away yet still dominating the landscape. Another reason for climbing early is to catch the morning calls of the gibbons

How Mengaris Punggor Got its Name

According to the elders of Kampung Bilit, an area known as Mengaris Punggor in the local language ("snapped Koompassia tree") was named after a fight between a snake and an elephant. The snake was coiled in this huge tree (the tallest in all the forest) when a passing elephant decided to grab it and pull it down. The snake held on tightly to the tree as the elephant tugged and tugged. The body of the snake stretched and stretched, but still it would not let go of the tree. The elephant also refused to give in and eventually their strength was such that the mighty tree snapped in half.

CEDE PRUDENTE

that frequent the forest nearby. Hearing their wonderfully clear yet somewhat haunting call ringing out over the forested hills has to be one of the most magical moments Borneo can offer.

The villagers of Bilit are enthusiastic supporters of their homestay programme, with more than one-third of the houses in the village involved (see page 99). Visitors can explore the oxbow lake, take early morning or late afternoon river safaris, learn traditional ways of fishing, help plant bananas for the elephants, climb Bukit Belanda, visit the traditional house, join in the daily volleyball game at the end of the day, help prepare the evening meal and enjoy watching a cultural show with local music and dance.

Electricity has only recently reached the Bilit, but not all homes have it so evenings are often spent chatting or recounting old tales rather than watching TV. You may hear some of the men say that during their youth, bears were much more frequent in the forests nearby. They claim that when bears climb a tree and start feasting on honey, they are so obsessed with this delicious treat that they ignore all else. A favourite dare which some of the men swear to have carried out when young was to touch the back of a bear while it was eating—before running away as fast as possible.

Kampung Sukau is the tourism hub of the lower Kinabatangan. Historically, this part of the river was an important trading centre because of its proximity to the Gomantong limestone caves and their priceless crop of edible birds' nests. Kampung Melapi, a village that existed near present-day Sukau, was home to Orang Sungei who had traditional rights to harvest the nests. When the British North Borneo Chartered Company began ruling the region in 1881, they claimed sole rights to the caves and their nests, understandably meeting considerable opposition from those who considered themselves the rightful owners. The headman of the village was eventually shot, and the trade in birds' nests re-routed through Bilit, 25 km upriver from Melapi.

Sukau and the adjoining village of Tomanggong is a picturesque settlement of around 2,000 Orang Sungei. The large wooden houses, raised high on stilts to avoid any floods, are generally surrounded by flowering shrubs and pot plants, and often shaded by large trees and with orchards behind. There's a real sense of civic pride, with both Sukau and Tomanggong kept clean and tidy. There is now an Information Centre in the middle of Sukau village, offering the use of computers to both locals and visitors—the age of the internet has indeed arrived in Sukau.

Due to the opening up of oil palm plantations in the region, there is an unsealed road leading from the main road to Lahad Datu, past the access road to Gomantong Caves and on to Sukau (about 39 km from the main road).

C.L. CHAN

Although the administrative centre of the Kinabatangan region is in Kota Kinabatangan (on the Lahad Datu road), Sukau offers adequate facilities for both locals and visitors. There is a simple restaurant, and basic supplies are available in several small shops, although few visitors actually come in to Sukau as almost all the wildlife lodges are located slightly upriver of the village, near a tributary, Sungei Menanggol.

At Sukau, the Kinabatangan flows wide and deep, even during the dry season. The Menanggol is a prime area for river cruises for wildlife viewing, where visitors are most likely to see a concentration of Proboscis monkeys (and, unfortunately, of other visitors). If limited wildlife is spotted here, the safari usually continues along the main river. The trees along the Menanggol are slightly lower than those along the Kinabatangan, and a boat moving slowly and quietly along the river during the late afternoon, shortly before sunset, is likely to encounter Proboscis monkeys, macaques and other wildlife, as well as many different birds.

It is impossible to predict what you will see, which is all part of the excitement of safaris along the river and to the nearby oxbow lakes. It could be a huge monitor lizard feeding on the carcass of a wild pig washed up on the river bank, an Oriental Darter diving to spear a fish right before your eyes, a mangrove snake lying immobile in a tree just overhead, a Buffy Fish Owl staring fixedly from a branch, a troop of macaques searching for crabs or even, if you're very lucky, a group of elephants congregating in a cleared area along the river bank.

Most tour companies offer a package which includes road transport from Sandakan, with a visit to Gomantong Caves en route for Sukau. This is followed by a late-afternoon river cruise for wildlife viewing, overnight at the lodge, a tour of an oxbow lake in the early morning, with return to Sandakan after lunch. However, to increase the opportunity of seeing a wide range of wildlife, a minimum two-nights' stay is preferable. The 3 day/2 night tour offered by most companies also includes jungle trekking along trails through the forest to oxbow lakes or hides nearby.

With the exception of Sipadan Dive Centre's beautifully constructed Proboscis

Wood and rattan ladders (left and p. 82) are used to climb to the cave roof to gather the birds' nests. Looking through a hole in the roof of Simud Hitam cave (below). A Buffy Fish Owl (opposite) is one of the several birds of prey which often haunt the area, waiting for tiny swiftlets or other easy game.

WENDY HUTTON

CEDE PRUDENTE

Lodge (which has chalets roofed in hardwood tiles and a large garden), and Borneo Eco Tours' lodge (which uses solar power and has a dining pavilion jutting over the river), Sukau's wildlife lodges are generally converted *kampung* houses, simple but comfortable wooden structures, sometimes with several small chalets built nearby. The lodges are renowned for their surprisingly good and abundant range of food, and most tour companies have knowledgeable wildlife guides who speak adequate English.

Apart from the lodges upriver from Sukau, North Borneo Safari offers a smaller and less expensive lodge in a beautiful riverside location immediately opposite a forested limestone hill, Bukit Tomanggong, just downriver from Sukau. A birding and wildlife trail has been made on the outcrop so that guests can explore the limestone and riverine forest, as well as enjoy a good view from the top of the hill.

A total of 10 homes have joined the Sukau Homestay Programme (see page 99 for details), which offers a range of activities including wildlife viewing and cultural shows, as well as food and accommodation in spacious and comfortable local homes.

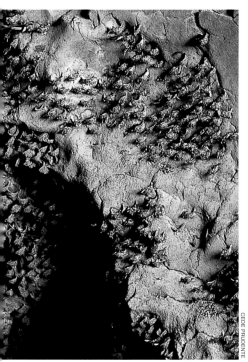

There are around ten limestone hills in the lower Kinabatangan, with plants especially adapted to the unique limestone environment. These hills fulfil an important function whenever the river floods, providing a safe haven for animals until the waters subside. Equally important, several limestone areas contain caves which are renowned for the edible birds' nests built by two species of swiftlet.

Gomantong Caves are located within the best known limestone outcrop in the lower Kinabatangan. This outcrop contains around nine caves and is the most important area for birds' nests in all of Sabah. To preserve the

Swiftlets (left) build their nests on the caves walls and roof. Collectors risk their lives (opposite) to gather these.

surrounding habitat for the swiftlets and bats which live in the caves, the caves are surrounded by the Gomantong Forest Reserve, where it is sometimes possible to spot orangutan, hornbills and red leaf monkeys (langgurs), as well as some interesting birds, including hornbills and several raptors and, sometimes, clouds of butterflies along the road in.

A clearly signposted road to Gomantong Caves leads off the main road to Sukau, 18 km away from its junction with the Lahad Datu road and about 40 minutes by road from Sukau. Visitors who are not on a group tour are required to register at the entry point, and can then drive along a sealed road

(a far cry from the almost impassable muddy track that existed a decade ago) right to the Reception Centre maintained by the Wildlife Department (see page 93 for entry times and fees). Although there are plans to develop an information centre and cafeteria next to the Reception Centre, at the time of writing no firm date was fixed.

Rare Slipper Orchids crow on the limestone outcrops (left). A model at Gomantong helps explain the gathering equipment (below).

S P LIM

WENDY HUTTON

A raised boardwalk leads through the forest (a welcome innovation during the rainy season) to the cleared area by the huge mouth of Simud Hitam, the only cave open to the public. During the harvesting seasons, the simple housing near the cave mouth is home to the workers employed by the contractor who pays a fee to the government for the right to harvest the nests. At other times, the quarters stand silent, some of the coiled rattan and ironwood ladders used to reach the nests during the harvest often stored underneath the building.

A boardwalk runs around the sides of the main chamber of the Simud Hitam cave, keeping visitors safe and clean above the thick layer of bat guano which teems with centipedes, scorpions, cockroaches and other insects, as well as helping protect the floor of the cave. Even when harvesting is not in progress, it is still a dramatic experience to visit the chamber and see the shafts of light coming through holes in the cave roof, and to hear the occasional disturbed bat squeaking.

All swiftlets make nests, but only two species create edible nests from their saliva, which hardens to form a tiny cup in which the female lays her eggs. The Chinese have believed for centuries that these nests have medicinal properties and, indeed, studies have shown that they contain a certain amount of some amino acids. They are so highly prized that the best quality "white" nests can fetch up to US$4,000 a kilo, while the so-called black nests (created by a different species of swiftlet, and containing some impurities which need to be removed) fetch around US$2,000 after cleaning.

The harvesting of the birds' nests is strictly controlled by the Wildlife Department to ensure its sustainability; indeed, the Gomantong Caves are claimed by international wildlife experts to be the best managed in the world. As soon as the swiftlets have built their nests in preparation for laying their eggs, the nests are collected. The swiftlets then create a second nest which is left undisturbed until the eggs have been laid, hatched and the young swiftlets have flown away. Once again, the harvesters move in to gather the now-empty nests.

Breeding seasons differ depending upon the actual caves in which the nests are made, and according to the variety of swiftlet. At Gomantong, the first harvest of the more valuable white nests in Simud Putih caves normally takes place in February, with the second harvest in June or July. Because access to Simud Putih is difficult, visitors are not permitted. However, the harvesting can be witnessed in Simud Hitam cave, generally in March or April, and then again in August or September. During the nest-making season, and while the eggs are hatching, each patch of nests within the caves is guarded around the clock to prevent any theft of this valuable commodity.

The sight of men risking their lives to reach into the nooks and crannies of the caves is unforgettable. Using a combination of a flexible rattan ladder and poles of rigid bamboo, the nest-gatherer climbs high up into the darkened recesses of the cave, using a sharpened stick to dislodge the nests, putting them into a woven basket which is eventually lowered down to the ground for emptying. All the time this is going on, other members in his team, guided by their experienced leader, shout out instructions, their cries echoing within the vast cave. Just near the entrance to the cave, there is a small-scale model of the paraphernalia used by the harvesters, which is very helpful in understanding just how the harvesting is carried out.

The river is the only route in to the village of **Kampung Abai**, the last settlement downriver, reminiscent of the past when boats were once the only method of access to all the villages along the Kinabatangan. Located on flat land on a sweeping bend in the river, Abai is located not far from brackish waters where only mangroves and nipah palms thrive.

The village was originally founded by 30 Sabangan families who migrated downriver, and were later joined by a number of Idahan from Lahad Datu. (The name of the village, Abai, means "to find" in the local language.) The population of Abai has declined in recent years, as families move to Sandakan or Sukau with their children when they finish the village primary school and need to go elsewhere for higher education. Today, although there are 82 houses in the village, many of them are unoccupied and the population has dropped from around 600 people to about half that number. Owing to its size, there is no restaurant in the village, although a small shop located on the ground floor of a local home offers basic supplies, including bottled water.

Sandakan, reached by boat through the channels cut through the mangrove swamps at the mouth of the Kinabatangan followed by a trip across the bay, is where most of the locals sell their fish, and where they buy

Johnsonville-on-the-Kinabatangan

In 1935, a wealthy (and, some might say, eccentric) American couple, Osa and Martin Johnson, came to the Kinabatangan to capture the local wildlife and natives on film, and to take back orangutan, gibbons and other wildlife for a zoo in New York. They built an entire village next to Kampung Abai, which they christened Johnsonville, as headquarters for themselves, their pilot, film sound engineer and other workers. The jungle was cleared, an electricity plant installed, six bungalows and a landing strip for their plane constructed, vegetable and flower gardens planted and various staff and animal quarters built. The Johnsons used this as their home for about one year, flying about the region in their own plane, which was also used for visits to Sandakan.

Some months after the Johnsons finished their filming and left for USA, Martin Johnson was killed in a plane crash. Rukke, coordinator of the Kampung Abai homestay, has compiled an oral history from interviews with elders who remembered the Johnsons, and hopes to build a small monument commemorating their year in the village.

MARTIN & OSA JOHNSON SAFARI MUSEUM

CEDE PRUDENTE

their major supplies. Depending on the size and speed of the boat, the journey from Abai to Sandakan can take from about 30 minutes to 3 hours.

Until relatively recently, most of the houses were roofed with thatch made from the nipah palm fronds readily available about 10 minutes downriver. Although picturesque, the nipah thatch is not as durable as corrugated zinc sheets, which now cover most of the houses. However, the cooking and eating area of almost every house is still roofed in thatch, which is significantly cooler, and it is here that a siesta is usually enjoyed during the hottest part of the day.

Perhaps partly because of their isolation, the villagers in Abai are particularly welcoming and friendly, and visitors will quickly feel like adopted family members. They may find themselves helping to sort and grade freshly caught river prawns, wrapping dough in banana leaf to make cakes, nursing one of the many babies, playing with the family cats or explaining to the local women that the cream many Westerners put on their body and face is sunscreen (which the local girls would love to be able to get their hands on).

Fishing is the sole livelihood in the Abai. Fish traps are fashioned from split bamboo, while cylindrical prawn traps are made of the abundant nipah fronds, with an interior cage of bamboo. During the rainy season, when the freshwater prawns are abundant, families can catch up to 40 kilos a night. These are graded according to size, and sold to fish dealers in Sandakan or upriver to the nearest oil palm estate. Fish are also caught in fixed nets (*pukat*) and sometimes cast nets are also used. The villagers supplement their staple diet of fish and rice with homegrown vegetables and fruits.

About 5 minutes by boat from Abai, the oxbow lake known as Danau Pitas or Danau Abai is perhaps the most beautiful of all the Kinabatangan lakes. Easily accessible by a channel off the Kinabatangan even during the dry season, the lake is constantly flushed by the tide and therefore lacks the algae often found in lakes with an outlet only during the rainy season. Danau Pitas is rich in birdlife with hornbills, egrets, the Oriental Darter, the rare Storm's Stork and kingfishers among the varieties which can be spotted.

The forest around the lake is a good place to view Proboscis monkeys at dusk, and it is also possible to catch sight of orangutan and elephants in the region. It may be possible to make arrangements to stay at Danau Pitas, while a homestay programme is in operation in Kampung Abai itself (see page 99 for further details).

CEDE PRUDENTE

C.L. Chan

Practical Information

WHEN TO VISIT

The Kinabatangan region can be visited all year round, although is often flooded during the wettest part of the year in December and January. The main flowering and fruiting season, from April to October, is generally fairly dry and a good time for spotting many birds and animals. During the northeast monsoon from November to March, there are often heavy showers during the afternoons, particularly during December and January. During the rainy season, however, it is possible to negotiate many of the river channels leading in to the oxbow lakes, where there is often a greater concentration of wildlife.

The first harvesting of birds' nests at Gomantong Caves generally lasts from February to April, and the second from August to September. March and August are perhaps the most reliable months to see the harvesters at work in the Simud Hitam cave, which is open to the public.

HOW TO REACH THE KINABATANGAN

Sandakan is the jumping off point for most visitors to the Kinabatangan; frequent daily flights from Kota Kinabalu to Sandakan, taking approximately 40 minutes, are operated by Malaysia Airlines. The standard return fare is RM188. AirAsia operates direct daily flights between Kuala Lumpur and Sandakan. Air-conditioned buses leave Kota Kinabalu for Sandakan and Lahad Datu from the bus station near the Padang from about 7 am daily; single fare is approximately RM30.

If using public transport to reach Sukau or Bilit, it is possible to take a mini-bus from

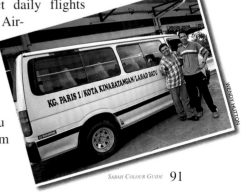

Sandakan. Most of these are "informal" and therefore not identified by the name of their destination painted on the side. Usually painted light cream, these leave from about 6 am until noon from in front of the Genting Mas supermarket opposite the local bus station in Jalan Pryer. A more flexible alternative is to take an air-conditioned bus to Lahad Datu from either Kota Kinabalu or Sandakan (or hail the bus in Labuk Road near Sepilok); travel only as far as the junction of the Gomantong/Sukau road, and from there, take one of the mini-buses waiting at the junction on to Sukau or Bilit (RM5). To return from Sukau to Sandakan, arrange in advance to book a seat in the mini-bus which leaves the village at 6.30 am (RM15).

An alternative way of travelling to Sukau is to take the ferry boat that leaves Sandakan harbour (from the jetty near the local bus terminal next to the main market) at 11 am daily. The boat takes about 1 $\frac{1}{2}$ hours to cross the bay to Suan Lamba, and costs RM3 (the return voyage departs at 5.30 pm).

WENDY HUTTON

From Suan Lamba, it is possible to take public transport in a van through an oil palm estate to the main road and on to Sukau; this takes about 1 $^1/_2$ hours and costs RM8.

Those driving across from Kota Kinabalu can travel to Gomantong Caves, Sukau and Batu Putih without going in to Sandakan. Turn into the road towards Lahad Datu at the busy junction known as Mile 32 (51 km before Sandakan); the road to Sukau/Gomantong, some 34 km away, is clearly sign-posted.

To reach Batu Putih, take a bus for Lahad Datu either from Kota Kinabalu or the main bus station at Mile 2.5 Jalan Labuk, Sandakan; alternatively hail one on Labuk Road near Sepilok or at the Mile 32 junction and get off at the Kinabatangan bridge.

Kampung Abai can be reached only by boat, either from Sandakan (arrange with SI Tours or with the homestay programme), or from Sukau (the return trip from Sukau will cost in the region of RM100).

ADMISSION TIMES AND FEES

Agop Batu Tulug

The entrance to the caves is clearly sign-posted on the main road, and an area set aside for parking. The caves are open daily, except Friday; admission is free but visitors are requested to register. The Information Centre is currently closed.

Kinabatangan Orangutan Conservation Project

For information on this project, and to arrange visits to discover orangutan in the wild near Sukau, contact HUTAN, tel (089) 230220 or (089) 230268, Email: hutan1@tm.net.my, or visit their office at Kg Tomanggong/Sukau.

Gomantong Caves

Access to the Simud Hitam cave within the Gomantong Forest Reserve is permitted from 8 am–6 pm daily. The entry fee is RM30 for non-Malaysians, RM5 for Malaysians. Video camera fee: RM50; Camera: RM30.

TOUR OPERATORS

All major tour operators in Sabah offer tours to the Kinabatangan region, with six of them maintaining lodges at Sukau. Most companies offer a cheaper rate to Malaysians and Sabah residents.

Borneo Eco Tours

12A, 2nd Floor, Lorong Bernam 3
Taman Soon Kiong, Jalan Kolam, Kota Kinabalu
Tel: (088) 234009; Fax: (088) 233688;
Email: info@borneoecotours.com;
Website: www.borneoecotours.com

This company's Sukau Rainforest Lodge has been recently upgraded, and now has an attractive dining pavilion right on the banks of the Kinabatangan, as well as a boardwalk discovery trail through the forest behind the lodge, where elephants can sometimes be seen. The cost of their well-managed tours (ex-Sandakan) is 2 days/1 night, RM625; 3 days/2 nights RM938 per person.

Discovery Tours

Room 908, 9th Floor, Wisma Khoo Siak Chew, Sandakan
Tel: (089) 274106; Fax: (089) 274107;
Email: distours@po.jaring.my;
Website: www.infosabah.com.my/discovery

Kota Kinabalu Office:
G22, Ground Floor, Wisma Sabah
Jalan Tun Razak, Kota Kinabalu
Tel: (088) 221244; Fax: (088) 221600

A large tour company with their main office in Kota Kinabalu, Discovery Tours maintains a wildlife lodge at Sukau, on the Kinabatangan.

North Borneo Safari Sdn Bhd

Lot 4, 1st Floor, Block 22, Bandar Indah, Sandakan
Tel: (089) 235525, (013) 856 0969; Fax: (089) 235526
Email: nbsafari@myjaring.net

This company, run by the pioneer guide in the Kinabatangan, maintains a lodge, downriver from the Sukau village. They specialise in the ground handling of wildlife photographers and documentary film makers. For the general visitor, they run bird and wildlife-viewing tours down the Kinabatangan to a tributary at Resang, as well as to the popular Menanggol river. The lodge consists of 10 simple twin-bed rooms, each with its own toilet & shower, located on the banks of the Kinabatangan River next to the office of the WWF Partners for Wetlands project. The location is beautiful and peaceful, with a riverside restaurant looking across to the limestone outcrop of Bukit Tomanggong. The 1 day/1 night package costs RM150 per person (minimum 2 persons); transfers between Sandakan or the airport and Sukau cost RM100 per person.

SI Tours Sdn Bhd

Lot 1002 & 1003, 10th Floor, Wisma Khoo Siak Chew
Lebuh Empat, Sandakan
Tel: (089) 213502/3, 223502
Fax: (089) 217807
Email: info@sitours.com.my;
Website: www.sitoursborneo.com

A special interest tour company which has won several awards, SI Tours conducts nature, culture and adventure tours to the Kinabatangan and Gomantong Caves.
Using their own fleet of boats, they offer a tour across Sandakan Bay and from the mouth of the Kinabatangan upriver to the settlement of Kg Abai. They maintain a lodge at Sukau. Their charge for Sukau trips, ex-Sandakan, is RM468 for 2 days/1 night (per person, on a twin-sharing basis) and RM568 for 3 days/2 nights, 1 night in Sukau and 1 night in a Kg Abai homestay.

Sipadan Dive Centre

Lot 1103, 11th Floor, Wisma Merdeka
Jalan Tun Razak, Kota Kinabalu
Tel: (088) 240584; Fax (088) 240415;
Email: sipadan@po.jaring.my;
Website: www.sipadandivers.com/proboscis
lodge

This company owns Sukau Proboscis Lodge, the most attractive lodge on the Kinabatangan, set in a large garden on the banks of the river not far from the Menanggol junction. Accommodation and the usual river tours and transfers are available at the lodge.

Wildlife Expeditions

Room 903, 9th Floor, Wisma Khoo Siak Chew,
Sandakan
Tel: (089) 219616; Fax: (089) 274331
Email: enquiry@wildlife-expeditions.com
Website: www.wildlife-expeditions.com
Kota Kinabalu Office:
Shopping Arcade, Ground Floor, Tanjung Wing,
Shangri-La's Tanjung Aru Resort,
Kota Kinabalu, Sabah
Tel: (088) 246000; Fax: (088) 231758;
Email: enquiry@wildlife-expeditions.com

Wildlife Expeditions was the first tour operator to open a lodge in Sukau. They now have 2 lodges; the original includes a number of chalets as well as the main building at the junction of the Menanggol river, while the more recent one is a kampung house located at the end of the small lane off the main road just before Sukau village.Their 2 day/1 night package ex-Sandakan, costs RM656 per person; the 3 day/2 night package costs RM818.

BOAT TRANSPORT

If you are not travelling on a package tour, you will need to arrange for boat transport to explore the Kinabatangan.

At **Kampung Abai**, **Kampung Bilit** and **Kampung Batu Putih**, the homestay programmes all offer boat service for wildlife viewing along the river and to nearby oxbow lakes.

Members of the **Sukau** boat owners' cooperative have established a set price, depending upon the size of the boat. A boat holding 6 persons charges RM60 for the entire boat for about 2 hours' wildlife viewing along the Kinabatangan and Menanggol rivers. Longer trips from Sukau downriver to Kampung Abai or upriver to Kampung Bilit are negotiable. Ask for Abdullah in Pak Karim's simple restaurant in the heart of Sukau village, opposite the village Information Centre, to help arrange boat hire. Alternatively, use the boat known as "Follow Me", run by Yusoff. He has a simple roadside shop on the right just before the entrance to Sukau village, with a yellow sign "Disini ada boat servis".

ACCOMMODATION

Batu Putih

The **Miso Walai** homestay programme at Batu Putih has been running since 2002 and is perhaps the best organised, with 21 families participating in 3 villages in the region. As well as providing food and accommodation, the homestay has a boat service and guides, and organises wildlife tours, camps, visits to their jungle lodge, cultural shows and handicraft demonstrations. The basic rate for food and accommodation is RM48, with extra for boat, guides and other services. Contact the Miso Walai Homestay project office, tel: (019) 813 9488; fax (089) 533 805; Email: tinjau@tm.net.my.

Danau Girang

Uncle Tan's Jungle Camp, located about 40 minutes downriver from the bridge at Batu Putih, offers accommodation consisting of several wooden huts with lino-covered floors, mattresses and mosquito nets. Basic bathroom and toilet facilities, thatch-roofed dining pavilions with good food and a friendly atmosphere, as well as a volleyball area. Transfers arranged from Uncle Tan's Bed & Breakfast, SUDC Shoplots, Mile 16 Jalan Labuk, Gum Gum, Sandakan; pickup from Sepilok is also possible. The basic 3 day/2 night package, including 2 or 3 river cruises per day and jungle trekking, plus transfer from Sandakan costs RM240. Camping overnight on an oxbow lake, Danau Usu is an option. Uncle Tan's also arranges for a 1-night extension at the Kampung Bilit Homestay. For reservations, tel: (089) 531 639; Email: eugene@uncletan.com; Website: www.uncletan.com

Kampung Bilit

The **Seratu Balai Homestay** at this village includes 10 homes with a capacity of a maximum 40 guests. The daily charge for 3 meals and accommodation is RM40 per person; guiding fees are RM20 per day, while a boat to the nearby oxbow lake costs RM50. The homestay is currently establishing a 3 day/2 night programme. To book, contact Jahidi, communications manager of the homestay, call: (019) 853 4997 or email: bilit2002@hotmail.com

Bilit Adventure Lodge, a large converted riverside house with 9 rooms accommodating 18 guests, is due to open towards the end of 2004. The accommodation and tours are operated by Sepilok Jungle Resort, tel (089) 533031, 533041, 533051; fax (089) 533029; e-mail: sepilokjr@yahoo.com.

Kampung Sukau

Initially, the only option for visitors wanting to experience the wildlife around Sukau was to take an organised tour and stay in a lodge owned or operated by the tour company. Recently, in an attempt to spread the tourism income more evenly among the local Orang Sungei, a homestay project and a boat owners' cooperative (which offers very reasonably priced guided tours) was established. There are also a few homes which are not part of the homestay programme which rent out rooms or an entire house, as well as offering boat service.

Sukau Homestay includes a total of 10 homes around Sukau village offering accommodation and 3 meals for RM40 per person per day. Additional activities including boat transport, guiding for wildlife viewing and cultural show are extra. For homestay bookings, contact Kinabatangan Orangutan Conservation Project (details p. 93).

Borneo Eco Tours, **Discovery Tours**, **SI Tours**, **Sipadan Dive Centre** and **Wildlife Expeditions** all maintain lodges at Sukau (see pages 94–97 for details). In addition, another small lodge operated by **North Borneo Safari** is available slightly downriver at Kampung Tomanggong. All lodges offer packages which include transport, accommodation, food and guiding services, and usually include a tour of Gomantong caves. See pages 94–97 for details of prices.

Kampung Abai

There are currently just 4 houses offering hospitality as part of the **Abai Homestay** programme. Owing to the remote location of the village, the lack of telephones and its accessibility only by boat, it may be easier to contact SI

Tours in Sandakan (see p. 96) for transport and coordination. Alternatively, write to the homestay coordinator, Rukke Mohd Yusoff, Kg Abai, WDT 274, 90009 Sandakan, or call his sister, Rozlina, at (089) 631935. Currently, RM35 is charged per person per night, with extra for food, wildlife tours or fishing trips with a guide, and a cultural show. Transport by boat to and from Sandakan (around RM400) on a locally owned boat can be arranged via the homestay coordinator, or booked through SI Tours in Sandakan.

Five minutes by boat from Kampung Abai, **ASAS Pemerhatian Unggas Kinabatangan** is located at Danau Pitas. Serious bird enthusiasts may be able to make arrangements to stay in the very simple accommodation right on the oxbow lake, to experience what is probably the richest area for birdlife in the entire Kinabatangan region. Contact Asnih Binti Etin, WDT 657, 90009 Sandakan, or email: asnih_etin@hotmail.com.

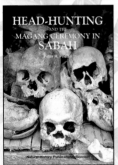

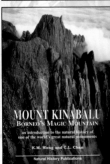

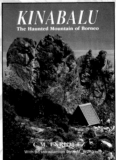

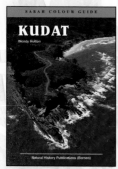

KUDAT

Wendy Hutton

Natural History Publications (Borneo)

古达

Wendy Hutton 陈贞 陈美玉 译

马来西亚自然史出版社

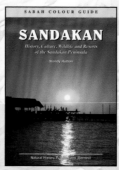

SANDAKAN

History, Culture, Wildlife and Resorts
of the Sandakan Peninsula

Wendy Hutton

Natural History Publications (Borneo)

山打根

历史·文化·野生动物
与旅游度假区

Wendy Hutton 陈贞 陈美玉 译

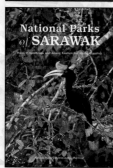

National Parks of SARAWAK

Hans P. Hazebroek and Abang Kashim bin Abang Morshidi

GUNUNG MULU NATIONAL PARK

Hans P. Hazebroek
and Dina Morshidi

MALIAU BASIN

SABAH'S LOST WORLD

Hans P. Hazebroek, Tengku Zainal Adlin
and Waidi Sinun

Natural History Publications (Borneo)

A Walk through the LOWLAND RAIN FOREST of Sabah

Elaine J.F. Campbell

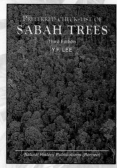

PREFERRED CHECK-LIST OF SABAH TREES

Third Edition

Y.F. LEE

Natural History Publications (Borneo)

IN BRUNEI FORESTS

An Introduction to the Plant Life of Brunei Darussalam

K.M. Wong
with watercolours by C.L. Chan

A Revised Edition

THE LARGER FUNGI OF BORNEO

David N. Pegler

Natural History Publications

RAFFLESIA OF THE WORLD

JAMILI NAIS

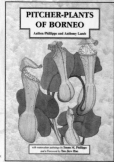

PITCHER-PLANTS OF BORNEO

Anthea Phillipps and Anthony Lamb

with watercolour paintings by Susan M. Phillipps
and a Foreword by Tan Jiew Hoe

NEPENTHES of BORNEO

CHARLES CLARKE

Natural History Publications

A GUIDE TO THE Pitcher Plants of Sabah

Charles Clarke

Natural History Publications (Borneo)

A GUIDE TO THE Pitcher Plants of Peninsular Malaysia

Charles Clarke

Natural History Publications (Borneo)

NEPENTHES
OF SUMATRA
AND PENINSULAR MALAYSIA
Charles Clarke

Natural History Publications (Borneo)

BORNEO
HUGO STEINER

ITS MOUNTAINS AND LOWLANDS
WITH THEIR PITCHER PLANTS
TREKKING FROM 1962 TO 2002

ORCHIDS
of SARAWAK
TEOFILA E. BEAMAN, JEFFREY J. WOOD,
REED S. BEAMAN AND JOHN H. BEAMAN

Natural History Publications (Borneo)
The Royal Botanic Gardens, Kew

ORCHIDS
of SUMATRA
J.B. COMBER

DENDROCHILUM
OF BORNEO
Jeffrey J. Wood

Natural History Publications (Borneo)
in association with
The Royal Botanic Gardens, Kew

THE PLANTS of
MOUNT KINABALU
3. GYMNOSPERMS AND NON-ORCHID MONOCOTYLEDONS

John H. Beaman and Reed S. Beaman

Natural History Publications (Borneo)
in association with
The Royal Botanic Gardens, Kew

THE PLANTS of
MOUNT KINABALU
4. DICOTYLEDON FAMILIES ACANTHACEAE TO LYTHRACEAE

John H. Beaman, Christiane Anderson and Reed S. Beaman

Natural History Publications (Borneo)
in association with
The Royal Botanic Gardens, Kew

The Genus
PAPHIOPEDILUM
Second Edition
Phillip Cribb

Natural History Publications (Borneo)
in association with
The Royal Botanic Gardens, Kew

SLIPPER ORCHIDS
OF BORNEO
Phillip Cribb

Natural History Publications

THE GENUS
COELOGYNE
A SYNOPSIS
Dudley Clayton

Natural History Publications (Borneo)
in association with
The Royal Botanic Gardens, Kew

ORCHID
CONSERVATION
Editors
Kingsley W. Dixon, Shelagh P. Kell,
Russell L. Barrett, Phillip J. Cribb

Natural History Publications (Borneo)

GINGERS
of PENINSULAR MALAYSIA
AND SINGAPORE
K. Larsen, H. Ibrahim, S.H. Khaw and L.G. Saw

Natural History Publications (Borneo)

MOSSES AND LIVERWORTS
of MOUNT KINABALU

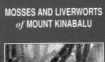

Jan Peter Frahm, Wolfgang Frey,
Harald Kürschner and Mario Menzel

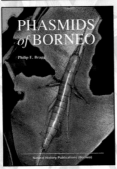

PHASMIDS
of BORNEO
Philip E. Bragg

Natural History Publications (Borneo)

An Illustrated Guide to the
STICK AND LEAF INSECTS
of Peninsular Malaysia and Singapore
FRANCIS SEOW-CHOEN

Natural History Publications (Borneo)

A GUIDE TO THE
DRAGONFLIES
OF BORNEO
THEIR IDENTIFICATION AND BIOLOGY
A.G. ORR
with colour photographs by
U. Norbiaisem

Natural History Publications (Borneo)

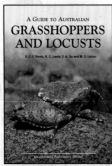
A GUIDE TO AUSTRALIAN
**GRASSHOPPERS
AND LOCUSTS**
D.C.F. Rentz, R.C. Lewis, Y.N. Su and M.S. Upton

Natural History Publications (Borneo)

The
BIRDS
of BORNEO
Fourth Edition
Revised by G.W.H. DAVISON
Natural History Publications (Borneo)
in association with The Sabah Society

The
BIRDS
of BURMA
Fourth Edition
Bertram E. Smythies
Natural History Publications (Borneo)

Swiftlets of Borneo
BUILDERS OF EDIBLE NESTS
Lim Chan Koon and Earl of Cranbrook
Natural History Publications (Borneo)

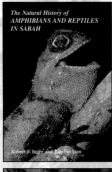
The Natural History of
ORANG-UTAN
Elizabeth L. Bennett
Natural History Publications (Borneo)

**PROBOSCIS MONKEYS
OF BORNEO**
Elizabeth L. Bennett and Francis Gombek

A Field Guide to the
FROGS OF BORNEO
Robert F. Inger
Robert B. Stuebing

Panduan Lapangan
KATAK-KATAK BORNEO
Robert F. Inger
Robert B. Stuebing
Disunting oleh
Anna Wong
Shahrul Anuar Mohd. Sah
Natural History Publications (Borneo)
Jabatan Muzium Sabah

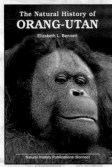
The Natural History of
**AMPHIBIANS AND REPTILES
IN SABAH**
Robert F. Inger and Tan Fui Lian

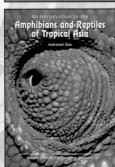
An Introduction to the
**Amphibians and Reptiles
of Tropical Asia**
Indraneil Das
Natural History Publications (Borneo)

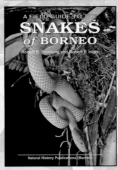
A FIELD GUIDE TO THE
SNAKES
of BORNEO
Robert B. Stuebing and Robert F. Inger
Natural History Publications (Borneo)

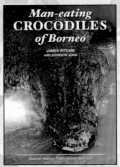
Man-eating
CROCODILES
of Borneo
JAMES RITCHIE
with JOHNSON JONG
Natural History Publications (Borneo)

TURTLES
of BORNEO
AND PENINSULAR MALAYSIA
Lim Boo Liat and Indraneil Das
Natural History Publications (Borneo)

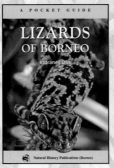
A POCKET GUIDE
**LIZARDS
OF BORNEO**
Indraneil Das
Natural History Publications (Borneo)

A POCKET GUIDE
**PITCHER PLANTS
OF SARAWAK**
Charles Clarke and Ch'ien Lee
Natural History Publications (Borneo)

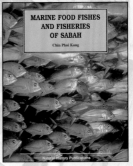
**MARINE FOOD FISHES
AND FISHERIES
OF SABAH**
Chin Phui Kong
Natural History Publications

THE FRESH-WATER FISHES OF NORTH BORNEO

ROBERT F. INGER AND CHIN PHUI KONG
With a Supplementary Chapter by Chin Phui Kong

Natural History Publications (Borneo)

LAYANG LAYANG
A Drop in the Ocean

Neonza Pilcher, Steve Oakley and Grissella Ismail

Natural History Publications (Borneo)

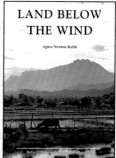

Three Came Home

Agnes Newton Keith

Natural History Publications (Borneo)

LAND BELOW THE WIND

Agnes Newton Keith

Natural History Publications (Borneo)

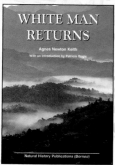

WHITE MAN RETURNS

Agnes Newton Keith

With an Introduction by Patricia Riggs

Natural History Publications (Borneo)

WITH THE WILD MEN OF
BORNEO

Elizabeth Mershon

Natural History Publications (Borneo)

FOREST LIFE AND ADVENTURES IN THE MALAY ARCHIPELAGO

Eric Mjöberg

Natural History Publications (Borneo)

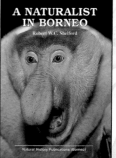

A NATURALIST IN BORNEO

Robert W.C. Shelford

Natural History Publications (Borneo)

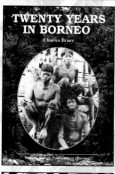

TWENTY YEARS IN BORNEO

Charles Bruce

Natural History Publications (Borneo)

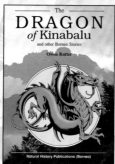

The
DRAGON of Kinabalu
and other Borneo Stories

Owen Rutter

Natural History Publications (Borneo)

A CULTURAL HERITAGE OF NORTH BORNEO
Animal Tales of Sabah

P. S. Shim
with illustrations by Yong Ket Hyun

Natural History Publications (Borneo)

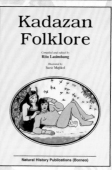

Kadazan Folklore

Compiled and edited by
Rita Lasimbang
Illustrated by
Suzie Majikol

Natural History Publications (Borneo)

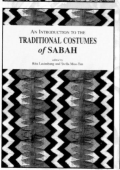

AN INTRODUCTION TO THE
TRADITIONAL COSTUMES of SABAH

edited by
Rita Lasimbang and Stella Moo-Tan

Etnobotani
GARY J. MARTIN
Diterjemah oleh Maryati Mohamed

SEBUAH MANUAL PEMULIHARAAN
'MANUSIA DAN TUMBUHAN'

Natural History Publications (Borneo)

Water Land Cities
Sabah, Malaysian Borneo

Sabah Tourism Board

51 Jalan Gaya, 88000 Kota Kinabalu, Sabah, Malaysia
Tel: 6088-212121 Fax: 6088-212075
Email: info@sabahtourism.com Website: www.sabahtourism.com